Thank You to all my lovely readers for taking time
book. You are amazing, unique, and so special.

This book is dedicated to all those who are connected
or wish to be connected to the beautiful continent of Africa.

I hope that when reading this book, you will be encouraged
to learn more about the beautiful and rich cultures that lie in Africa.

Always aspire to learn more about yourself, your roots and your native
language. Never lose touch of who you are and strive to have an
open mind, which allows you to learn more.

Flag of the
Democratic Republic of Congo

*Follow the blue text
in the story to read in Lingala!

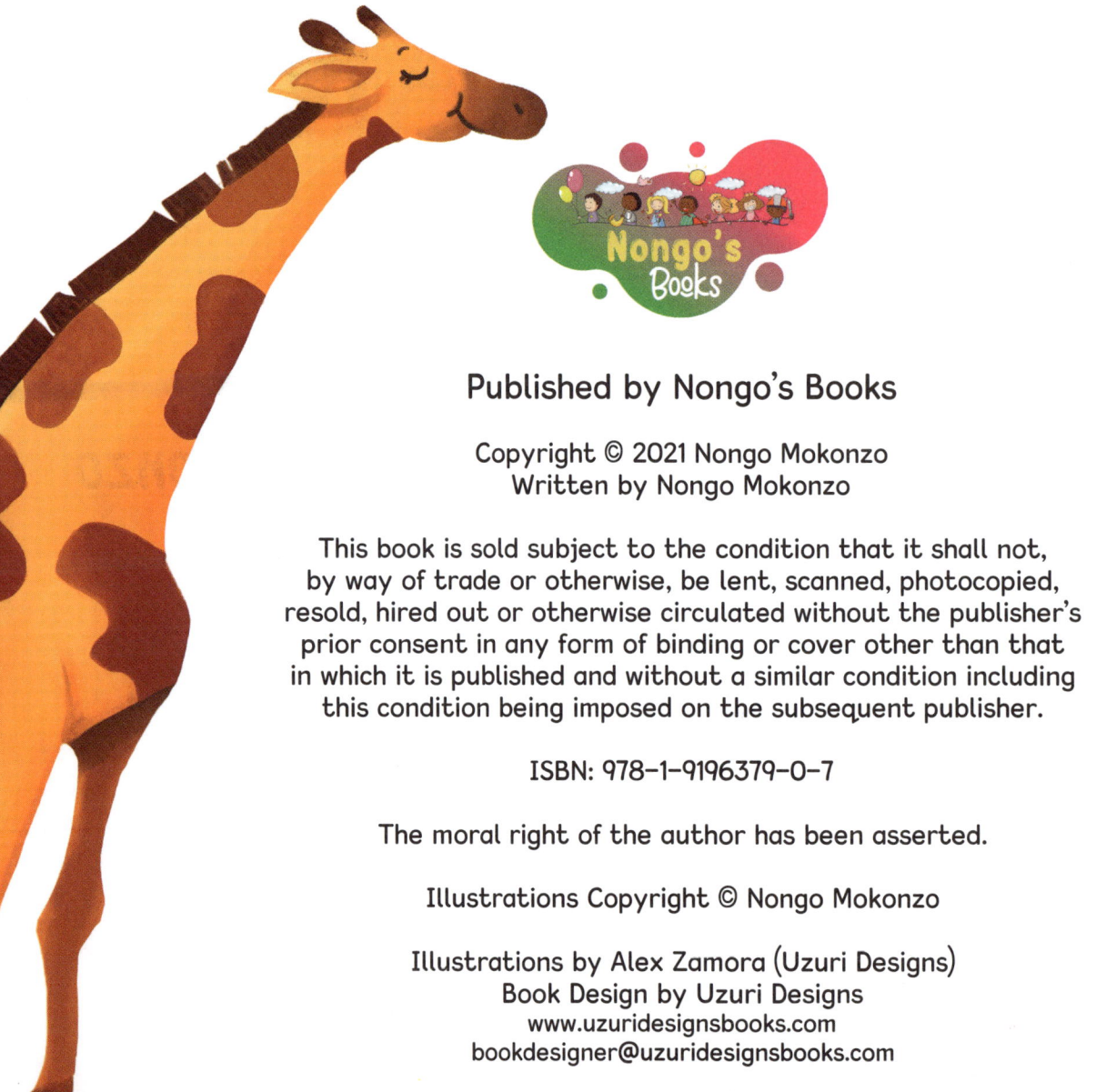

Published by Nongo's Books

Copyright © 2021 Nongo Mokonzo
Written by Nongo Mokonzo

This book is sold subject to the condition that it shall not, by way of trade or otherwise, be lent, scanned, photocopied, resold, hired out or otherwise circulated without the publisher's prior consent in any form of binding or cover other than that in which it is published and without a similar condition including this condition being imposed on the subsequent publisher.

ISBN: 978-1-9196379-0-7

The moral right of the author has been asserted.

Illustrations Copyright © Nongo Mokonzo

Illustrations by Alex Zamora (Uzuri Designs)
Book Design by Uzuri Designs
www.uzuridesignsbooks.com
bookdesigner@uzuridesignsbooks.com

ANIMALS OF OUR LAND

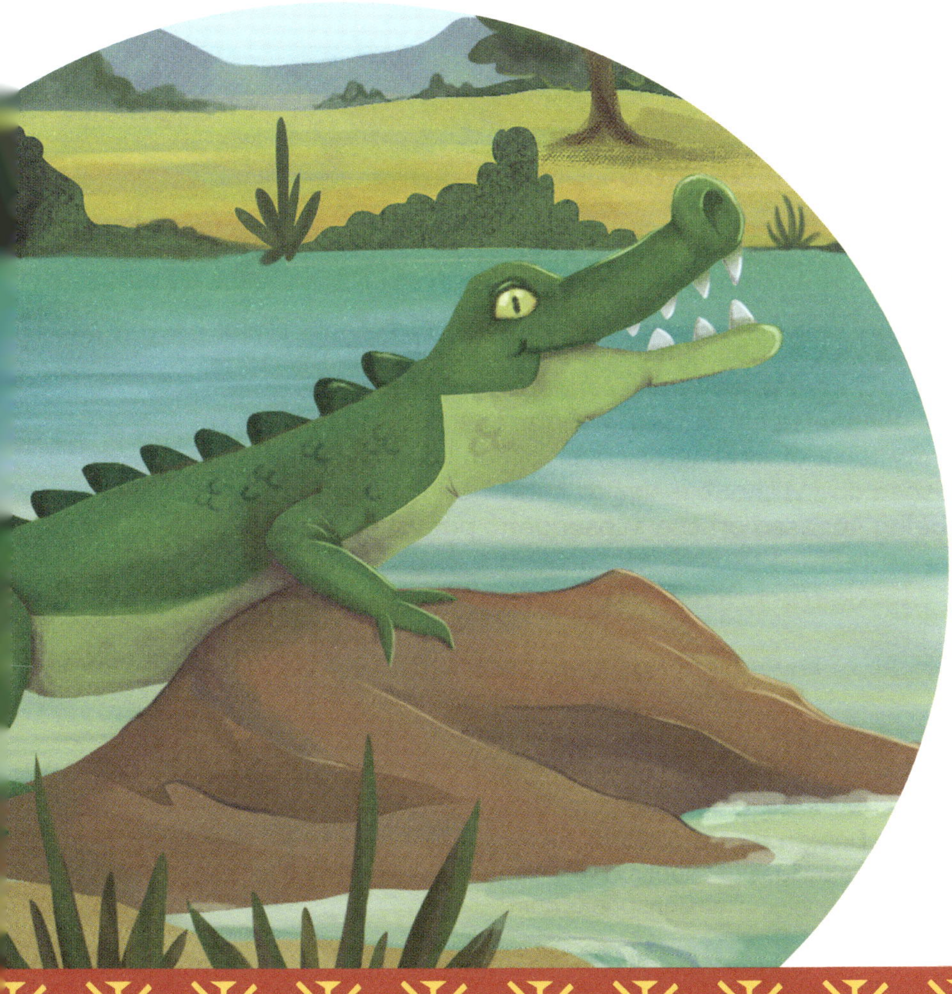

Written By
Nongo Mokonzo

Meet the Mokonzo Family

**Mum
Nongo**

**Dad
Eric**

Jeremiah

Azariah

Isaiah

Zechariah

Amariah

Adoniah

The Mokonzos are a Congolese family who live in the United Kingdom.

The parents and the children are on an adventure in the DR Congo.

They are visiting the wildlife to learn the names of these animals in Lingala.

They would like you to come on this journey with them and learn their mother tongue.

This is a giraffe.
A giraffe has a long neck.

Oyo ezali nkema.
Nkema bazali mayele.

This is a monkey.
Monkeys are intelligent.

This is a chicken.
Chickens make lots of noise.

Oyo ezali mokomboso.
Mikomboso bazali makasi.

This is a gorilla.
Gorillas are strong.

Oyo ezali nkosi.
Bankosi bagangaka makasi.

This is a lion.
Lions roar loudly.

Oyo ezali nkoyi.
Nkoyi bazali na loposo kitoko.

This is a leopard.
Leopards have very
beautiful fur.

Oyo ezali mondonga.
Mondongo bazali na loposo
moindo na mpembe.

This is a bird.
Birds fly high in the sky.

This is a fish.
Fishes live in the sea.

Oyo ezali nzoku.
Nzoku baza na matoyi minene.

This is an African elephant.
African elephants have big ears.

"Mum, Dad this has been so interesting, we have learned so many animal names in Lingala, we need to practice how to pronounce them."

"Yes kids, the more you practice, the better; you will always know your mother tongue."

Thank you for coming on this journey with us. See you soon!

Acknowledgements

To my loving husband Eric Mokonzo, thank you for your continuous support, for being my rock, for motivating and believing in me.

Thank you to my children, for being my reason to believe I can and will achieve anything I put my mind to. You are the energy and the motivation for this book.

To my parents, Mrs. Lily and Mr Jean-Pierre Ifeko for being the best parents and my biggest supporters.

To my in-laws, Gérard and Mrs Mariam Mokonzo, thank you for your contribution of ideas, your knowledge and your wisdom.

Thank you to Christelle and Ezekiel Leye for all your efforts to help and contribute your ideas.

Thank you, Naomi Yfeko for supporting
my ideas and your encouraging words.

I would also like to thank Gloria Kabamba for
cheering me on and always believing in me.

Thank you, Brenda Tukei, for your insight and aiding in the process,
your positive words, and your constant support.

Thank you, Benite Dibateza, for your limitless
resources that I found very insightful.

Thank you, Cassandra Bowen, for your consistent hard work.
It has been an honour and pleasure working with you.

Thank you, Alex Zamora, for your beautiful illustrations,
which has made the book come to life.

Nongo Mokonzo